FAMOUS PEOPLE

Bill Gates

by Adam Woog

KIDHAVEN
PRESS™

THOMSON
GALE

San Diego • Detroit • New York • San Francisco • Cleveland
New Haven, Conn. • Waterville, Maine • London • Munich

© 2003 by KidHaven Press. KidHaven Press is an imprint of The Gale Group, Inc., a division of Thomson Learning, Inc.

KidHaven™ and Thomson Learning™ are trademarks used herein under license.

For more information, contact
KidHaven Press
27500 Drake Rd.
Farmington Hills, MI 48331-3535
Or you can visit our Internet site at http://www.gale.com

LIBRARY OF CONGRESS CATALOGING-IN-PUBLICATION DATA

Woog, Adam, 1953–
    Bill Gates / by Adam Woog.
    p. cm. — (Famous people)
Includes index.
Summary: Examines the life of Bill Gates, his early interest in computers, the founding of Microsoft, his success as a businessman, his family life and philanthropic activities.
Includes bibliographical references and index.
  ISBN 0-7377-1400-X (hardback: alk. paper)
1. Gates, Bill, 1955– 2. Microsoft Corporation—History—Juvenile literature.
3. Computer software industry—United States—History—Juvenile literature.
[1. Gates, Bill, 1955– 2. Businessmen. 3. Microsoft Corporation—History. 4. Computer software industry.] I. Title. II. Series.
  HD9696.2.U62 G378 2003
  338.7'610053'092—dc21

                                                          2002008897

Printed in the United States of America

CONTENTS

INTRODUCTION

A Need to Win

In some ways, Bill Gates is an ordinary person. He grew up in a close-knit family. He works hard and likes to relax with games, books, and movies. He is married and has children.

In other ways, however, Gates is unusual. He is the cofounder and chairperson of Microsoft, the world's biggest computer **software** company. Microsoft has more than forty thousand employees in sixty countries. Gates is also one of the richest people in the world. His personal fortune is estimated at more than $50 billion.

Gates is not just a rich businessperson, however. He is also an important inventor. He was a key figure in the computer revolution of the 1980s, and he still plays a major role in controlling the direction of computing.

The Computer Revolution

Today, personal computers are so common that it is hard to imagine life without them. The computer revolution of the 1980s made it possible for the world to send, receive, store, and handle information in new ways. It also changed the way people learn, play, work, and live.

When Bill Gates was a boy, computers were huge, clumsy, and expensive. Only a few experts knew how to use them. They were not part of everyday life.

That changed in the 1970s. One big reason was the development of microcomputers. These desktop-sized machines were the ancestors of today's personal computers, or PCs.

At first, microcomputers were only interesting toys. However, Gates and his friend Paul Allen sensed their power. While still teenagers, Gates and Allen wrote the first really useful software programs.

This software was useful only for computer scientists and hobbyists. But then the computer revolution began, and ordinary people discovered how useful and fun computers could be.

Millions of people began buying computers. Microsoft software ran most of these machines. Today, most of the world's personal computers still use Microsoft products. Gates's often-repeated motto—"A computer on every desk and in every home, each running Microsoft software"—is close to reality.

Bill Gates, inventor and businessman, is cofounder of Microsoft, the world's largest computer software company.

Supersmart

In the computer revolution's early years, Gates was often called a boy genius for his programming abilities. Now he is known as a business genius for his ability to keep Microsoft ahead of its competition.

Gates himself prefers the term "supersmart." He does not think of himself as a genius. He says, "If you're any good at math at all, you understand business. It's not its own deep, deep subject."[1]

Gates has always known that he is intelligent, however. As a child, he was cruelly sarcastic if other people were not as quick as he was. He is still legendary for his temper and sarcasm if something does not meet his standards.

Gates craves constant information. He once wanted to learn African place names, so he put a map on his garage wall. His eyes swept the map every time he got in or out of his car. Not even those few small moments passed without input.

But he is not simply a walking brain. He has a mischievous side, enjoys active sports, and has tremendous physical energy. He has so much energy that he often rocks quickly back and forth while talking or thinking.

Gates has been successful thanks to a combination of intelligence and energy, hard work and good luck. Perhaps above all, Gates also has a strong need to win. This mixture of characteristics has been in him since he was very young.

CHAPTER ONE

Boy Meets Computer

William Henry Gates III was born in Seattle, Washington, on October 28, 1955. His mother, Mary, a schoolteacher, was very involved in community service. His father, Bill Gates II, was a lawyer.

When Bill was born, his grandmother, who loved playing cards, nicknamed him Trey. Trey means "three" to card players. It showed that he was the third William Henry Gates. The nickname stuck, and Bill's family still calls him Trey.

Math, Science, and Bargaining

As a boy, Bill had lots of energy. He liked tennis and waterskiing. He also enjoyed Boy Scouts.

However, Bill was also clumsy, small, and skinny. As a result, his parents considered holding him back in school. Bill's teachers persuaded Bill's parents that he should stay with his age level.

Even as a child, Bill was bright. He loved reading about many subjects. By age nine, he had read the entire *World Book Encyclopedia*. He also loved fiction books such as *Charlotte's Web*.

Bill loved math and science, and he always earned top grades in these subjects. In the fourth and fifth grades, he listed "scientist" as his future job.

When he was eleven, Bill showed a skill he would later need—the ability to write contracts. His first contract gave him unlimited use of his older sister Kristianne's baseball glove in exchange for $5. The contract read: "When Trey wants the mitt, he gets it."[2]

A Good Environment

Bill worked hard and studied hard. He spent hours in the school library after class, helping the librarian track lost books. When his class was given an hour to write a report on the human body, most of his classmates wrote one page. Bill wrote fourteen pages. His childhood friend Carl Edmark remembers, "Everything Bill did, he did to the max. What he did always went well, well beyond everyone else."[3]

Bill's parents encouraged his intelligence and hard work. They enjoyed lively conversations at dinner.

Bill (shown here at age eight) was a bright child who loved to read.

They also encouraged competition through games and word contests.

Bill's parents even used a game to tell their children that another child was due. During a game of hangman, they wrote: "A little visitor is coming soon." Bill's younger sister, Libby, was born in 1964.

Bill's grandmother was helpful as well. Gam, as she was called, often played games such as bridge with him and his older sister. To their grandmother, the games were tests of skill and intelligence. Bill's mother recalled, "She was always saying to him, 'Think smart! Think smart!'"[4]

As an adult, Bill has often remarked on how lucky he was to have a close-knit, competitive, and smart family. He says it helped him develop into the person he is now.

Discovering Computers

In his last years of elementary school, Bill had some problems. He seemed immature for his age, and he was bored with school. When he was finished with the sixth grade, his parents decided to send him to Lakeside, a private, all-boys school to continue his education.

Bill liked Lakeside, mostly because the classes were challenging. He still did poorly in subjects that bored him, however. He kept a B average but earned As in math and science.

At the beginning of eighth grade, in 1968, Bill returned to Lakeside and discovered something new. The school had a **teletype** machine.

Bill acted like most teenagers, talking on the phone and eating lots of pizza.

This device connected to a huge computer, called a **mainframe**, elsewhere in the city. Lakeside bought time on the mainframe to do simple computing.

By today's standards, this setup seems ancient. In 1968, however, it was new and exciting. Bill recalls, "There was just something neat about the machine. I realized later part of the appeal was that here was an enormous, expensive, grown-up machine and we, the kids, could control it."[5]

Tic-Tac-Toe
Bill showed a deep understanding of computing right away. The Lakeside teacher in charge of it joked that Bill passed him in knowledge of the machine within a week.

The first program Bill wrote made the computer perform simple mathematical formulas. The second was a tic-tac-toe game. It was very slow. It often took a full lunch period for the machine to play one game.

Buying time on the mainframe was expensive, and the students quickly spent their budget. Luckily, they found a solution.

The company that owned the mainframe was Computer Center Corporation, or C Cubed. Its mainframe was as big as a refrigerator and cost millions of dollars.

The computer was unreliable, however. Even with constant care, it broke often. C Cubed needed somebody who could find and fix its **bugs**. The company asked the Lakeside kids to do this. They were paid in blocks of free computer time.

First Jobs

During Bill's senior year, he and a friend, Paul Allen, built a computer for themselves. They formed a company, Traf-O-Data, to make money by processing data about traffic patterns.

The company was not successful, mainly because the computer was unreliable. However, Traf-O-Data gave Bill good experience in computing and in business.

Later that year, a large company, TRW, hired the two friends as programmers. TRW needed a program to help it monitor electricity from dams. Bill's parents and teachers let him do the work as a senior project.

Gates and childhood friend Paul Allen (right) would use their early computer experiences to develop Microsoft.

The project ran far behind schedule. At the TRW offices in southwest Washington State, Bill and Paul worked nonstop. They survived on pizza and Tang.

The TRW experience was both good and bad. It was good because Bill completed a large, complex project and worked with top engineers. It was bad because it showed him how not to run a company.

TRW thought any problem could be solved with extra people and more money. Bill saw that fewer people, working efficiently, could do the same job faster

Harvard University's historic clock tower. Gates became a Harvard student in the fall of 1973.

and cheaper. "We swore to ourselves that we would do better,"[6] he later recalled.

At College

During his senior year, Bill was accepted to Harvard University, in Cambridge, Massachusetts. He began there in the fall of 1973.

Bill had always been the best math student in school. At Harvard, he met people who were just as good or better than he was. It was a humbling experience. Yet Bill still excelled at computer studies.

Bill was an odd figure at Harvard. Although he liked to play poker, he was not interested in typical student pastimes such as music, dating, or drinking. He rarely bothered to bathe, and he did laundry as little as possible. He often ate only hamburgers and pizza, and stayed up many nights studying or writing computer programs. According to legend, he seldom put sheets on his bed.

His friend Paul Allen, meanwhile, had taken a job with an electronics company in Boston, near Harvard. He and Bill stayed in close touch. Soon, they started a project that would change their lives.

CHAPTER TWO

Starting
Microsoft

I n December 1974, Allen bought the newest issue of *Popular Electronics*. This magazine featured an exciting new device. It was a blue box with thirty-six lights and twenty-five switches.

It was the Altair 8800, the first affordable microcomputer. (The term "personal computer" had not yet been invented.) The Altair 8800 was manufactured by Micro Instrumentation and Telemetry Systems (MITS) of Albuquerque, New Mexico.

Today, the Altair seems primitive compared with even a simple pocket calculator. At the time, though, it had an amazing 64 kilobytes of memory and 256 **bytes** (not megabytes) of RAM. It cost $397 unassembled, or $498 assembled.

Programming the Altair required hours of flipping switches. If any one of hundreds of commands was done incorrectly, the machine shut down. Even if the programming was done perfectly, all the machine did was blink its lights on and off in sequence.

The Altair had serious limitations. The worst was that it had no language. Users could not "talk" to the computer. Without a language, the Altair was only a toy. It could not be used to create useful or interesting programs.

Improving the Altair

Gates and Allen decided to write a language. They thought they could adapt **BASIC** (Beginner's All-purpose Symbolic Instruction Code). This was a relatively simple language already used with large mainframe computers.

The two realized they needed to move fast, however. They knew that other people would have the same idea. Bill recalls thinking, "Geez, we'd better get going, because we know these machines are going to be popular."[7]

So they contacted MITS and said they that they already had a version of BASIC that would run on the Altair. This was not entirely true, however. Gates and Allen had only the idea, not the actual version.

The owners of MITS were interested. A meeting was set up for the following month. Gates and Allen then put in thirty days of nonstop activity, creating what they claimed they already had. Bill's lengthy sessions in the Harvard computer lab were "hard-core"—a phrase he later made famous. "Hard-core"

Gates is pictured with a computer in the early 1980s, around the time he and Allen became big names in the software business.

meant that every moment was devoted to the project. Gates often slept on the floor of the lab. Sometimes he fell asleep at his keyboard, then woke up and immediately started typing again.

When the language was finished and stored on punched paper tape, Allen flew with it to Albuquerque. He went because he looked more mature than Gates. The teenagers thought Allen would make a better impression than the boyish-looking Gates.

2+2=Microsoft

When Allen nervously instructed the MITS machine to run his program, paper tape began streaming through its reader. After fifteen minutes, the computer's printer finally clacked out a return message: MEMORY SIZE?

He typed in the amount of memory and the computer responded by writing READY. Paul typed in PRINT 2+2, and the answer came back: 4.

It worked! MITS liked it and wanted to work with the two programmers. Elated, Allen returned to Boston to deliver the good news. He moved right away to Albuquerque and took a job with MITS. Gates took a leave of absence from school and followed Allen a few months later. Their plan was to form a company to write languages for the Altair and other microcomputers. To start it, they each contributed some savings—a total of about $1,500. Officially formed in the summer of 1975, the company was first called Micro-Soft, then MicroSoft. Within a few months, the two founders settled on its now-familiar spelling, Microsoft.

Gates spent long hours in front of the computer writing the first BASIC program for MITS.

Gates takes a quick break from working. He is surrounded by computers in his Microsoft office.

Other Clients

MS-BASIC, as their first product was called, was sent out with every new Altair. Microsoft received a small royalty (fee) with every copy.

However, Gates knew that other companies besides MITS were developing microcomputers. All of them would need software. So he negotiated a nonexclusive contract with MITS. This meant that Microsoft could license MS-BASIC to other companies.

Gates also knew that Microsoft was not the only company writing software for microcomputers. He wanted to beat this competition.

His plan was to make his product so cheap that every computer manufacturer would choose it. He later wrote, "We didn't want to give anyone a reason to look elsewhere. We wanted choosing Microsoft software to be a no-brainer."[8]

The plan worked. Contracts with several big companies gave important boosts to Microsoft. Soon, nearly every top brand of microcomputer used a version of MS-BASIC.

Business was so good that Gates and Allen hired several more people to help. In 1976 Allen quit MITS and started working at Microsoft full time. Soon after, Gates dropped out of Harvard. His family was upset at this decision, but he was excited.

Allen and Gates pose with some of the many computers that use their Microsoft software.

Business Style

From the beginning, Microsoft's founders had different interests and skills. Allen looked at the big picture, focusing on new ideas and the future of technology. Gates was more concerned with everyday, practical business.

Gates had always been an independent thinker and a hard worker. His style became the standard at Microsoft. He expected employees to do their jobs without much guidance. Needing help was seen as a sign of weakness or ignorance. He also expected everyone to work as hard as he did. Seventy-hour workweeks were not unusual.

Gates's casual personal style also influenced other Microsofties, as the company's few other employees called themselves. Dress was informal.

The company's secretary, Miriam Lubow, was in her forties, much older than the other Microsofties. She was more than just a secretary; she was also Gates's personal assistant. She made sure he ate properly, slept enough, bathed and changed clothes, and got to the airport for business trips with more than a few minutes to spare.

Leaving Albuquerque

As Gates signed more contracts with computer makers, Microsoft became less reliant on MITS. There was little reason to stay in New Mexico.

Gates and Allen considered moving to northern California, which was already the home of many

Executives Jon Shirley (left) and Steve Ballmer (right) help Gates (center) handle the business side of Microsoft.

computer-related firms. However, they decided to return to the Seattle area. They and several other Microsofties were Pacific Northwest natives. They missed the trees, mountains, and water, and they missed their families.

Late in 1978 Microsoft relocated. The company's new offices were in Bellevue, east of Seattle. Bill rented a house for himself in the Seattle neighborhood where he had grown up. The move marked the beginning of a new era.

CHAPTER
THREE

Playing
to Win

In the early 1980s, as Microsoft settled into its new home, many changes were happening with computers. Microcomputers were now called personal computers, or PCs. The machines were becoming easier to use. Millions of nonexperts such as secretaries, businesspeople, and lawyers began buying them. All of these people needed software. Microsoft began selling directly to the public.

At the same time, many different manufacturers were making PCs. One was IBM, the biggest computer manufacturer in the world. For years, IBM had dominated the market in manufacturing mainframe computers. When Gates struck a deal to provide software for IBM's PC, it changed computing forever.

The pairing of IBM and Microsoft was an odd match. The giant, conservative **hardware** company,

A technician works with an early model IBM computer in 1969. By the 1980s, IBM had become the biggest computer maker in the world.

nicknamed Big Blue, was so different from the tiny, casual software company. At an early meeting, one IBM engineer mistook Gates for an office boy. The engineer could not believe that the head of a growing company looked like a high school kid in a sweatshirt.

At another meeting, IBM's engineers mentioned that their planned PC needed an **operating system**.

Operating systems control the overall function of a computer and do much of the unseen work for other programs. Gates recommended a California company. When that did not work out, Gates boldly suggested that he could supply IBM's operating system.

This was an enormous job, but also a wonderful opportunity. IBM was such a big company that if its operating system was successful, other companies would copy its design. IBM wanted to set the standard in personal computing. Gates wanted to help set that standard so that he could sell his operating system to other firms.

86-DOS

Many people doubted that Microsoft could create an operating system in less than a year. Gates and Allen, however, had a plan.

They knew that a Seattle programmer, Tim Paterson, had already developed an operating system that needed only some modification. It was called 86-**DOS** (for Digital Operating System). Microsoft bought it for $75,000 and renamed it MS-DOS.

To modify it, Gates and his team put in "hardcore" work sessions. Fourteen-hour days, six or even seven days a week, were normal. Everyone survived on hamburgers and the free sodas that were (and still are) a Microsoft tradition.

They made their deadline, and Big Blue released the IBM PC in August 1981. It was a hit. Millions were bought, each with a copy of MS-DOS. Microsoft received money for each computer sold.

Paul Allen after his retirement from Microsoft.

Meanwhile, Gates's prediction about IBM setting the standard was correct. Other companies began copying IBM's **hardware**. This was relatively easy to do. However, no one could copy MS-DOS, so each company had to license it from Microsoft.

Within a few years, MS-DOS was the operating system for most PCs around the world. Microsoft's sales boomed, and by 1982 the company that started with only twenty-eight employees had around two hundred.

Allen Leaves

In 1982 Gates lost the partner he had worked with since high school. Paul Allen was diagnosed with a form of cancer. Fortunately, it was treatable and he recovered.

However, the episode deeply affected Allen. He realized that there were many things he wanted to do in life but had put aside because of work. He retired from Microsoft.

Gate was worried about Allen's illness and deeply unhappy about his leaving. However, Gates pushed on with new projects. One of them, Windows, was an operating system designed to replace MS-DOS.

Windows was very different from MS-DOS. MS-DOS used clumsy, slow keyboard commands. Windows used a mouse, a pointer, and screen icons to form a **graphical user interface**, or GUI.

Windows Arrives

Gates promised that Windows would be even better than MS-DOS. However, it took a long time to create. Reporters began making fun of Gates. They called Windows "vaporware," meaning a promised product that never appears.

In 1985 Windows was finally presented to the public. This was over a year and a half after its original release date.

At first, the new system had many problems. It was slow and full of bugs, and little software was available for it. Also, it was the focus of a lawsuit by Apple Computer.

Apple argued that Microsoft stole the GUI idea from an operating system designed for its new Macintosh computers. Gates replied that the basic idea for the GUI had been done years earlier by another com-

*Gates holds a Microsoft Windows disk. Windows put
Microsoft at the forefront of the computer industry.*

pany. He said, "I think it's more like we both have this
rich neighbor . . . and you broke in to steal the TV set,
and you found out I'd been there first and you said,
'Hey, that's no fair! I wanted to steal the TV set!'"[9]

Many experts thought that, overall, Windows was
a flop. However, Gates persisted to push his product.
Later versions improved and Gates has promoted
each with multimillion-dollar ad campaigns. As a result,

The Microsoft corporate headquarters rests among four hundred acres of lawns and gardens in Redmond, Washington.

Windows remains the primary operating system for PCs.

Celebrity

Gates was already well known within the computer industry, but during the 1980s he became famous among the general public. Microsoft's public relations department worked hard to make its "boy genius" a celebrity. Soon, the public identified him more closely than anyone else with the booming PC revolution.

In 1983 Gates was named one of *People* magazine's "25 most intriguing people." In 1984 he was on the cover of *Time*, and *Esquire* named him one of the "best of the new generation."

Microsoft kept growing, meanwhile. In 1984 it became the first software company to reach yearly sales of $100 million. It also swelled to seven hundred employees. Gates knew he needed a more permanent arrangement for these workers than cramped office space. He bought four hundred acres of land in nearby Redmond and had several buildings constructed. The company moved there early in 1986.

The new location was like a pleasant college campus. Lawns and gardens separated the buildings. Almost everyone had a private office, and many had an outside view.

Big Bucks

Soon after the move, Gates became a millionaire many times over. This happened when Microsoft stock began selling on the stock market. Gates sold some of his shares, but kept enough to own 45 percent of the company. This allowed him to keep control of his company and its products.

Microsoft stock rose quickly, and by 1987 Gates was the youngest billionaire in history (not counting those who inherited wealth). That same year, Microsoft became the world's biggest software company.

During the late 1980s, Gates's public image began to slip. He had once been known as a boyish genius and a brilliant businessperson. However, the media and general public began criticizing him.

Some critics simply resented his wealth and fame. Many others, however, resented his need to win at any

cost. They accused Gates of unfairly dominating the competition, of buying up small companies to gain their products, or even of sabotaging any new technology that threatened Microsoft. These critics compared Gates to the ruthless industrialists of earlier times.

Gates generally paid no attention to his critics. He argued that he was simply a smart businessperson. He has continued to take this stand into the present day.

CHAPTER FOUR

Businessperson, Family Man, Philanthropist

For most of his adult life, Gates focused almost completely on business. He had a reputation for thinking about little else, and for never giving up.

For years, Gates rarely took vacations or even day-long breaks. He even disconnected his car radio and refused to own a TV, because he felt they were distracting.

However, in recent years Gates's focus has changed. His life now includes relaxation, family, and philanthropy—that is, donating money to worthy causes. Gates says that he will keep working as long as it is fun. But he is also spending time on other pursuits.

Private Life

Gates was so focused on business that for a long time he did not have a steady girlfriend. He went out with women occasionally, but he had no regular girlfriends

After years of thinking only about business, Gates's interests turned to family and other pursuits.

until 1984. That year, he began seriously dating Ann Winblad, a software executive from Minnesota.

The two both led busy lives, but they managed to be together fairly regularly. If they were in separate cities, they sometimes had what they called "virtual dates." They would go to the same movie at about the same time, talking on their car phones before and after the movie.

Winblad and Gates broke up in 1987. The next year Gates began dating Melinda French, a Texas-born Microsoft product manager.

Gates's friends agreed that the two were well matched. Like Gates, French was focused and smart. She was also funny and charming. They said her charm offset some of Gates's sarcasm.

One difference between the two was that French was health conscious. She regularly worked out, and she liked to eat a more balanced diet than Gates's regular routine of hamburgers and pizza.

Marriage

The couple dated off and on for several years. Gates's mother, Mary, liked French very much. She half jokingly told her son that he was taking too long to settle down.

The issue turned serious when Mary Gates developed breast cancer. Gates's romance may have been sped up by his mother's illness. She wanted to see him wed before she became seriously ill.

Gates proposed, and French accepted, while they were on vacation. Gates diverted their chartered jet to

Bill Gates and his wife, Melinda. The couple married on January 1, 1994, after several years of dating.

Omaha, Nebraska, the home of his friend, investor Warren Buffett. Buffett arranged for a jewelry store to open on a Sunday morning so that they could choose a ring.

The couple was married on January 1, 1994, on the Hawaiian island of Lanai. One hundred thirty guests filled the island's hotels for a week before the wedding. The festivities included New Year's Eve fireworks and a surprise appearance by Willie Nelson, Melinda's favorite musician.

Gates's mother was at the ceremony. A few days later, however, she entered a Seattle hospital. She died in June. In honor of Mary Gates's many years of community service, the city of Seattle named a street after her.

The Family Home

Melinda quit Microsoft after the wedding. Their first child, Jennifer Katharine Gates, was born in 1996. Gates joked that something else besides his competitors kept him up at night. Another child, Rory John Gates, was born in 1999, and a third child is expected in 2002.

Melinda Gates now devotes much of her time to a charitable foundation she and her husband founded. By all accounts, she does her best to downplay the fact that she is one of the richest women in the world. Although the family takes security precautions, she is sometimes spotted doing normal tasks such as grocery shopping or dropping off her children at school.

With his new family to consider, Gates began working more on something he had started years earlier: the construction of a high-tech house with an estimated cost of about $50 million.

The house is located in Medina, a waterfront neighborhood near the Microsoft campus. It is huge—about as big as twenty average American homes put together. From the outside, however, it looks like five normal wooden houses. Much of it is hidden or underground.

Taking Care of Business

Marriage and house building did not distract Gates from keeping his company going strong. Despite his reputation as a sharp businessperson, however, Gates sometimes made mistakes. The Internet, for instance, nearly passed him by.

The Gates family lives on the shore of Lake Washington. Gates's high-tech home cost about $50 million to build.

In the Internet's early days, no one knew how important it would become. Gates more or less ignored it. However, by 1994 millions of people were surfing the Net with **browsers** such as Netscape. Gates decided to develop his own browser. Even with a late start, Microsoft's browser, Internet Explorer, became a serious rival to existing browsers.

Another business problem for Gates in recent years has been a complex legal battle. The government is investigating claims that Microsoft has been breaking laws guaranteeing fair competition.

Gates argued that his company has always been fair, and that other companies simply have not been as smart. He made fun of these rivals. He told reporters, "In the future, maybe our competitors will decide to become more competent."[10]

Giving It Away

Compared with other wealthy men, Gates did not contribute much to charity in his early years as a tycoon. He said that he wanted to concentrate fully on building his business.

However, he also said that he would eventually focus, just as hard, on giving his money away. Recently, he has begun to fulfill this promise. Some observers note that Melinda Gates is the primary force behind this change. She oversees much of their philanthropy.

Gates's donations have included millions of dollars to schools such as the University of Washington and Harvard University. He and Paul Allen also funded a science building at their old high school, Lakeside. It is called the Allen/Gates Science Center. Allen's name

Gates, his wife, and his father, William Gates II, get ready for a groundbreaking ceremony for the University of Washington's new law school building.

Bill Gates is likely to influence the computer industry for years to come.

appears first because Gates lost the coin toss to determine that.

Gates's largest donations, however, have been for global health and education. These are made through the Bill & Melinda Gates Foundation. The Gateses have committed more than $21 billion to this organization. So far, the foundation has donated about $3 billion to worthy causes.

Gates has forever changed the computing world. There is little doubt that he will play a major role in the future of computing. There is equally little doubt that he will use his money and power to help guide the future of world issues, such as world health and education.

NOTES

Introduction: A Need to Win

1. Quoted in Randall E. Stross, *The Microsoft Way.* Reading, MA: Addison-Wesley, 1996, p. 47.

Chapter One: Boy Meets Computer

2. Quoted in Stephen Manes and Paul Andrews, *Gates: How Microsoft's Mogul Reinvented an Industry—and Made Himself the Richest Man in America.* New York: Doubleday, 1993, p. 21.
3. Quoted in James Wallace and Jim Erickson, *Hard Drive: Bill Gates and the Making of the Microsoft Empire.* New York: John Wiley, 1992, p. 12.
4. Quoted in Manes and Andrews, *Gates*, p. 18.
5. Bill Gates, *The Road Ahead.* New York: Viking, 1995, p. 1.
6. Quoted in Susan Lammers, *Programmers at Work.* Redmond, WA: Microsoft Press, 1986, p. 80.

Chapter Two: Starting Microsoft

7. Quoted in Lammers, *Programmers at Work*, p. 79.
8. Gates, *The Road Ahead*, p. 44.

Chapter Three: Playing to Win

9. Quoted in Manes and Andrews, *Gates*, p. 225.

Chapter Four: Businessperson, Family Man, Philanthropist

10. Quoted in Wallace and Erickson, *Hard Drive*, p. 55.

GLOSSARY

BASIC: Beginner's All-purpose Symbolic Instruction Code. An early programming language.

browsers: Software allowing people to surf the Internet.

bugs: Problems in computer software or hardware.

bytes: Units of measurement for computer memory. One byte equals eight bits. A bit is the smallest unit of information that a computer can store.

DOS: Disk Operating System. One version, MS-DOS, became the most common operating system for computers.

graphical user interface (GUI): An operating system that uses a mouse and screen icons, rather than just keyboard commands, to control a computer.

hardware: The physical components of a computer.

mainframe: A large computer.

operating system: A program that controls all the basic functions of a computer.

software: Instructions (programs) that tell a computer what to do.

teletype: An early device used to transmit electronic information from one location to another, and to print it out.

FOR FURTHER EXPLORATION

Sara Barton-Wood, *Bill Gates, Computer Legend.* Austin, TX: Raintree, 2002. Aside from some misspelled names and other minor mistakes, this book has excellent color photos and a simple, clear text.

Aaron Boyd, *Smart Money: The Story of Bill Gates.* Greensboro, NC: Morgan Reynolds, 1995. A good, clearly written biography.

Joan D. Dickinson, *Bill Gates, Billionaire Computer Genius.* Springfield, NJ: Enslow Publishers, 1997. A well-organized and well-written book for young adults, including good quotes and sources.

Jeanne M. Lesinski, *Bill Gates.* Minneapolis, MN: Lerner Publications, 2000. A book for young adults written in connection with the A&E network's *Biography* series. Contains some good photographs.

INDEX

PICTURE CREDITS

About the Author

Adam Woog has written more than thirty books for adults, young adults, and children. He lives with his wife and daughter in his hometown of Seattle. He wrote this book using Microsoft Word and an iMac.